Pocahontas

A stage play for fourth-year English pupils

by
Thomas Scherer

Cornelsen

Pocahontas

von
Thomas Scherer, Jockgrim

Verlagsredaktion
Ursula Fleischhauer

Technische Umsetzung
Harald Kertz

Grafik
Roy Schofield

Cornelsen online

http://www.cornelsen.de

1. Auflage € Druck 6 5 4 3 Jahr 06 05 04 03

Druck: CS-Druck CornelsenStürtz, Berlin

ISBN 3-464-06815-3

Bestellnummer 68153

Gedruckt auf säurefreiem Papier, umweltschonend hergestellt aus chlorfrei gebleichten Faserstoffen.

Contents

Foreword

Pocahontas is a play designed to be read and enjoyed – and performed – by fourth-year English pupils.

The story presented here is by no means historically accurate, although I have consulted two biographies of Pocahontas as well as Captain Smith's *General History of Virginia*. For the purpose of the play, however, I had to select and rearrange certain events, and obviously I had to keep the language and content within the intellectual range (extensive though that may be) of learners aged 14 - 15.

I would like to ask forgiveness for certain liberties I have taken with the documented facts, and for some minor clichés. A case in point: tobacco had been known to Europeans for many years before the English settled in Jamestown, Virginia, in 1607. For the sake of fun I have introduced tobacco as a novelty in the play.

The Powhatans were a powerful tribe in the Tidewater area of Virginia. They spoke an Algonquian dialect, of which quite a few words, like "wigwam"and "tomahawk", have survived. (The origin of "OK" is uncertain, but granted that it was used by the natives, it has become by far the most popular "Indian" word in modern English.)

The early settlers had problems with Indian names: Powhatan is the name of the tribe (or confederacy of tribes) whose head chief at the time was also called Powhatan, though his real name probably was Wassuhonacock. By the same token, Pocahontas is the name which the chief gave his favourite daughter, whose clan name is reported as Matoaka.

Thomas Scherer

The characters

(15 speaking parts and several non-speaking parts)

- Pocahontas (alias Matoaka, alias Rebecca)
- Captain John Smith
- Powhatan (alias Wassuhonacock)
- John Rolfe
- Matachanna, Pocahontas' sister
- A medicine man

English settlers:
- Alan
- Barry
- Charlie
- David
- Edward (an old man)
- Francis
- George
- Harry
- Miss Needle

Indian warriors and squaws

Scene: The English colony of Virginia, from 1607 to 1622

Prologue

Pocahontas approaches from rear stage with a basket full of corn-cobs. She walks slowly up to front stage, kneels down offering the corn, then drops the basket and covers her face with her hands while the following text is spoken (from pre-recorded cassette) with the sound of drums in the background:

The morning of April 26, 1607 changed my world for ever. I did not know that date then. I did not even know the date of my birthday. I only knew that I was Matoaka, a young girl of 12 winters, the favourite daughter of Wassuhonacock, who was the leader of our people. The world I knew then was the world of my people, the Powhatans. We lived together in the village of Werowocomoco, which looked like a big and safe place to me then. It was a peaceful life, and I believed it would go on like that for ever. I would some day marry one of my people and raise corn and children in the homeland of the Powhatans.

But on that morning we saw something we had never seen before. We saw trees that came from the sea to our coast. One hand was not enough to count them. When they came nearer we realized that what we saw were three canoes much bigger than our wigwams. We had never seen a canoe that big. We did not know who was on the three canoes, but we were sure that the people who swam on them must be very special people, very powerful people. We did not know what to expect. Some of us were afraid, some of us got excited. We all knew that something very important was going to happen. However, not a single one of us expected that our lives would be changed completely and for ever.

Scene one

While the players come on stage to take their places and arrange the stage props, one player presents a signboard on which is written:

WINTER 1607
The Natives give a helping hand
When English settlers take their land.

Five settlers are sitting around a campfire with a kettle on it. Their clothes are shabby and dirty. They are cold and hungry and very angry about their present condition.

Alan: What a terrible place! Will this winter never end? I'm freezing and as hungry as a wolf.

Charlie: If I had known, I would never have come here.

Barry: Back in London, they promised us "mountains of gold". Pshaw! I couldn't find one gram of the stuff. And I've been all over the country.

David: Yeah, we've looked everywhere, but no luck!

Alan: Forget the gold. What we need now is something good to eat. I'm tired of digging up roots and stuff. I would gladly pay ten pounds for a piece of meat!

David: If you had any money.

Charlie: And if there was any meat.

Edward: Back in England, it was even worse. We didn't have anything to eat at all. We were lucky if we could cook the sole of a shoe!

Barry: Well, you're lucky now. We've got the sole of my boot in our stew, and it's nearly ready to eat. *(He fishes the sole out of the kettle with his fork.)*

Captain Smith: *(returning with his gun from a hunting trip)* Well, men, how are you doing?

Alan: Badly, Captain, badly. If we don't die of hunger, the cold will get us in the end.

Captain Smith: If you had built houses in time instead of hunting for gold, you would be a lot more comfortable now.

David: Yeah, but what about food?

Captain Smith: That's **your** problem. I told you to plant corn, but you wouldn't listen. You ran away to look for gold. And look what you've got now!

Charlie: Is there no chance left, Captain? You think we can't survive?

Captain Smith: I'm not saying that, but things look pretty bad. With all that snow it's hard to hunt wild animals.

Edward: Back in England, it was even worse. It got so cold the birds froze in the air.

Barry: And you caught them in the frying-pan when they dropped from the sky? Ha, ha.

Francis: *(running on stage)* The redskins are coming! The redskins are coming!

All: What? Where? How many?

Captain Smith: Have your arms ready, men. But remember: don't shoot unless they start shooting first!

David: If we don't fight, those devils will take our scalps!

Barry: What would they want your scalp for? It's full of lice.

They get ready to defend themselves.

Charlie: I don't want to be killed – or worse: to be burned alive at the stake! They do terrible things to their prisoners.

Edward: Back in England, the Indians were even more terrible ...

Alan: Oh, shut up, silly. There are no Indians in England.

Edward: So what? The aristocrats are as bad.

Captain Smith: Stop arguing. Here they come.

The Powhatans appear. The men are wearing leather shirts and leggings, the women long leather dresses. Their faces are not painted. There are no ornaments in their hair; only the chief wears a "crown" of feathers.

Powhatan: Wingapoh.

Captain Smith: How do you do, Chief. You must be Powhatan.

Powhatan: *(points at his followers)* Powhatan. *(points at himself)* Wassuhonacock.

Barry: What? Hen or cock? I didn't catch the name.

Captain Smith: *(points)* Me – Captain Smith. They – English.

Powhatan: Yangis?

David: Why doesn't he speak plain English? I don't understand a word.

The chief makes a sign. Some Indian girls approach with baskets full of corn-cobs, turkeys and other food.

Barry: *(seeing the corn)* Gold!

Captain Smith: You are wrong. This is much better than gold. It's the food we need to survive. *(to the chief)* Thank you. *(They shake hands.)* I hope that from now on we will be friends. Friends – you understand? *(He makes signs.)*

Powhatan: Howgh.

He takes out his peace-pipe, sits down and fills it. Smith sits next to him.

Alan: My, those girls are pretty!

Charlie: True, but I don't like the way the warriors keep watching them.

The girls hand food to the hungry men. Powhatan and Smith smoke the peace-pipe. It is handed on to the men, who take turns smoking.

David: Arrgh! This is like putting your head in the chimney!

Alan: *(refusing the pipe)* Terrible stuff! It's called tobacco, I believe.

Charlie: If you ask me, this stuff will never be used by white people. Never!

Barry: Are you sure? I think it tastes quite nice.

Alan: You like that taste? Now I can understand why you wouldn't mind eating the sole of your shoe!

Barry: *(pointing at Pocahontas)* I wonder who that girl is. She looks special. Almost like a princess.

Charlie: A princess? She's probably just some Indian squaw.

Powhatan: Matoaka! *(She goes to him.)* Pocahontas. *(= my favourite daughter)*

Captain Smith: Pleased to meet you, Pocahontas.

Pocahontas: Pleasemeechu.

Captain Smith: You speak English?

Pocahontas: *(shakes her head and uses signs)* You – me – Yangis.

Captain Smith: You want me to teach you English? Fine. But you must teach me some of your language, too.

Pocahontas: *(hands him some corn and beans)* Succotash.

Captain Smith: We call this corn. Or rather: Indian corn.

Pocahontas: Indian?

Captain Smith: You – Indian!

Pocahontas: No. Me – Powhatan.

Captain Smith: All right, all right. You probably don't know that you are an Indian. All you know is that the name of your tribe is Powhatan.

They eat.

Pocahontas: OK?

Captain Smith: What?

Pocahontas: *(points at corn, rubs stomach)* OK?

Captain Smith: Oh, yes. "OK". I guess that is what they say when they mean "all right".

David: Why don't they say "all right" then, like everybody else?

Alan:	Well, it's their language.
David:	But it sounds funny. This is "OK", that is "OK"! We'll soon talk like these Indians!

John Rolfe comes back from the hunt.

Captain Smith:	Well, John, we have visitors. Did you get any game?
John Rolfe:	No. But as I can see, you've got all the food you need now.
Captain Smith:	John, meet Wasu..., meet the chief of the Powhatans. *(They shake hands.)* And this is his daughter, Pocahontas.
Pocahontas:	Pleasemeechu.
John Rolfe:	I've never seen an Indian girl like you. You must be a princess.
Captain Smith:	Come, John, have some food. The Powhatans were kind enough to help us.
John Rolfe:	Food? I don't feel like eating now.
Captain Smith:	What's wrong with you? Are you ill?
John Rolfe:	No, eh – yes, just a little. What a beauty!
Captain Smith:	*(holding a turkey up by its legs)* Yes, isn't it? It must weigh more than ten pounds.
John Rolfe:	I'm not talking about the turkey.

Captain Smith: Well, John, if you mean Pocahontas – don't forget that she's not a Christian girl.

John Rolfe: That can be changed.

Captain Smith: You want to become a missionary?

John Rolfe: I would become anything for that girl.

Captain Smith: Why, John, you are in love!

John Rolfe: Don't tell anyone about it, Captain.

Captain Smith: Trust me. *(He shakes his hand.)* Men, let's have a feast of thanksgiving tonight: the English and their Indian friends will celebrate together!

All: Hooray!

Scene two

The white man's god has come to rule,
His red children go to Sunday school.

An Indian village

A young girl, Pocahontas' sister Matachanna, is lying on a "bed" on the floor. She is ill. The medicine man is dancing around her, rattling a gourd. He is painted wildly and wears a fantastic headdress of horns and feathers. Other Indians are sitting quietly in the background, softly banging their drums.

Medicine man: Ha–ya–ya–ya!

Pocahontas enters with John. She points at the Bible he is carrying.

Pocahontas: She – bad spirit. You – good book.

John Rolfe: But I can't heal this girl with the Bible. She is ill, you know, sick.

Pocahontas: Yes, ill – much ill. You heal Matachanna, OK?

John Rolfe: You don't understand. This book heals the spirit, not the body.

Pocahontas: Yes, heal spirit. This girl – bad spirit.

John Rolfe: I can see that she is very ill. But I'm not a doctor.

Pocahontas: You doctor. You have good book.

John Rolfe: I can pray for your sister if that is what you want. Can you send this man away? He's getting on my nerves.

Pocahontas: Sssh!

The medicine man becomes quiet and – as in a trance – slowly dances away. They go to the sick girl.

John Rolfe: *(touches her forehead)* She has a high temperature.

Pocahontas: You take bad spirit away?

John Rolfe: No, I'm only taking her temperature. *(He looks her over.)* Well, she's got some willow bark around her legs. That will probably help to reduce the fever. And what is this? *(He smells at some jar near the head of the patient.)* Smells like herb tea. Well, your medicine man does a lot of hocus-pocus, to be sure, but I imagine he knows more about healing than I do.

Pocahontas: No good. You take book.

John Rolfe: This book is not magic, Pocahontas. But it's got the good spirit in it. Come, let's pray together. *(They kneel down to pray.)* Our Father, which art in heaven ...

The drums get louder.

John Rolfe: I wonder how anybody can get well with all that noise. Let's go away.

Pocahontas: She – well again?

John Rolfe: Let's hope she will be well soon.

They move away. Matachanna is carried off stage on her bed.

John Rolfe: Listen, Pocahontas, we white people have some powerful medicine, as you say, but we get ill and die, too. The big difference is in what we believe.

Pocahontas: Yes, your god – in book; our god – all around us.

John Rolfe: No, no, you don't get the point. God has made this world for us.

Pocahontas: Is that true?

John Rolfe: Yes, every word in this book is true. We must carry out God's will on earth, and then we can go to heaven.

Pocahontas: Is heaven – nice place?

John Rolfe: Well, no one knows what it looks like, but it's promised in the book that there is no war, no pain, no hunger in heaven.

Pocahontas: Is heaven far from here?

John Rolfe: Yes, very far. Actually, you must die to get there.

Pocahontas: Then I no want to go there. Is day so beautiful. *(She dances around and turns a cartwheel.)*

John Rolfe: But your sister Matachanna might want to go there.

Pocahontas: *(sits down again, sadly)* So you think she – die?

John Rolfe: Oh, I don't mean that. What I mean is: if she dies now without being a Christian, she can't go to heaven.

Pocahontas: No heaven for Matachanna?

John Rolfe: I'm sorry. And that is why I want you to become a Christian soon. The idea that you could not get to heaven one day really makes me sad.

Pocahontas: You – good man, John.

John: Oh, Pocahontas, you know that I care for you a lot. But I think I would love you even more if you became one of us. You understand? I want you to become a good Christian woman.

Pocahontas: *(touches his arm)* You teach me. *(They leave.)*

Scene three

1612
Paths of war cross paths of love:
The eagle grabs the gentle dove.

In the woods
Two English scouts approach cautiously with their guns.

George: You really think the Indians are serious about going on the warpath?

Harry: Of course. I've always known it: we'll never be friends with the Indians. And I'm fed up with them. Why don't we drive them away for good?

George: Don't forget: they helped us when we were in big trouble.

Harry: Yes, but since then the Indians themselves have been our biggest trouble.

George: We haven't been very nice to them either.

Harry: That's because the Indians lie and steal. And they are the laziest people alive.

George: Didn't they help you build your hut?

Harry: Yes, but that was years ago. Anyway, they don't need the land like we do. If they don't go away in peace, we'll just have to kill them.

George: Now be careful. The captain told us not to shoot or hurt anyone, unless they start fighting first.

Harry: That's not my idea of a war. Strike first, or the enemy will get you in the end.

They walk away. Pocahontas and her sister appear with baskets full of berries.

Matachanna: Don't walk so far, Matoaka. The woods have become dangerous.

Pocahontas: Everybody talks of war. But my heart is at peace.

Matachanna: Good for you. But our people are very angry with the whites because the Yangis lie and steal. And they are the greediest people alive. They want all our land.

Pocahontas: There is enough land for all of us. We should not fight each other, but learn from each other, and live together in peace.

Matachanna: I don't think that is possible. If we want to live in peace, we'll have to kill them.

Pocahontas: Kill them? Don't talk like that. Actually, the whites are nice people.

Matachanna: Nice people?! They almost killed one of our brothers when he took an old knife from them without asking first.

Pocahontas: There are bad people in every nation: in the Yangi nation as well as in the Powhatan nation. But there are many good people on both sides, believe me.

Matachanna: You must be thinking of your friend John. I agree he is a fine man. But what can he do alone against all the others? *(Pocahontas covers her face with her hands.)* Come, now. Maybe you're right. We should learn their way of life and ... *(she hesitates)*

Pocahontas: And what?

Matachanna: Marry our women to their men.

Pocahontas: Why not? Let me tell you: I've become a Christian and I want to become John's wife.

Matachanna: I hope you will be happy. *(They embrace.)*

The scouts return.

Harry: Hey, look who's there!

George: Two Indian squaws. You don't want to fight against girls, do you?

Harry: Of course not. But don't you recognize the one on the left?

George: Why, that's Pocahontas, isn't it?

Harry: Right. And you know what? We'll kidnap the girls and take them to our village.

George: I see. When we have the chief's daughter, we can use her to bargain with the Indians.

Harry: You've got it. Now, let's move quietly.

They approach the two girls and jump on them.

Harry: No sound, or you're dead. *(The girls are too shocked to move.)* Quick, let's tie them up. *(This can be done in mime play. Ropes are not really necessary.)*

George: Keep still. *(Matachanna tries to free herself.)*

Harry: Let's get out of here. Didn't I say we should "strike first"? We've done it!

They run off with their prisoners.

Scene four

To make war one man will do;
To make peace there must be two.

In the settlers' village
Harry and George arrive with their prisoners.

Harry: Well, Captain, what do you think of this?

Captain Smith: Did I tell you to do this? Untie them. *(They do so.)*

Harry: But Captain ...

Captain Smith: We are not fighting against women.

George: Now look, that's not the idea.

Captain Smith: What is the idea?

Pocahontas: Captain Smith, if your men had not brought me here, I would have come on my own.

Captain Smith: You are a brave girl, Pocahontas.

Matachanna: Brave? I think she is a fool. But if you plan to kill us, we will die like Powhatan warriors. You will not hear a sound from our lips nor see a tear in our eyes.

Captain Smith: Nobody here is going to kill you, or hurt you.

Pocahontas: Listen to me, Captain Smith. My people want to go on the warpath.

Captain Smith: Well, we are prepared.

Pocahontas: But fighting is no good. Many people will get killed, white people, Indian people.

Captain Smith: I know, but what should we do?

Pocahontas: Talk to my father. He has learnt to speak your language. And he can also speak to his own people.

Harry: And don't forget: the old man will soon find out that we've got his daughter in our power.

Captain Smith: Quiet, please. Carry on, Pocahontas.

Pocahontas: We must find a way of living in peace together.

Matachanna: How can you talk like that? These Yangis don't want peace. They carried us here like sacks of potatoes. Now they can do with us what they want.

Pocahontas: Hush! Captain Smith is a good man.

Captain Smith: I hope so, although I'm not sure that I'll be able to help you. There's been too much trouble, and it will be difficult to stop people from fighting.

Harry: If Powhatan loves his daughter, he'll think twice about attacking us.

Captain Smith: Didn't I tell you to shut up? Now, if you don't mind, you'll stay here with us, Pocahontas, and we'll send your sister back to your father's village to invite Powhatan over for a meeting. OK?

Pocahontas: OK.

Matachanna: I'll go, but I'm sad at heart.

Captain Smith: Don't worry. I promise that we won't touch the chief. He can come and go as a free man, and he can take his daughter back home – whatever his tribe decides to do.

Matachanna: I hope you'll keep your promise.

Pocahontas: Go ahead, Matachanna, and fetch our father. I'm sure everything will end well. *(Matachanna leaves.)*

Harry: Hell, it looks like the captain is giving away our advantage.

George: What do you mean? If we could make peace, that would be wonderful.

Harry: Maybe. But just think of this: as long as we've got the chief's favourite daughter in our power, we can ask for almost anything.

George: You mean all the land we want?

Harry: Of course. The Indians don't believe that they own the land anyway. So they won't mind too much giving some of it away for the life of a young girl. *(They walk away.)*

Rolfe appears and tries to console Pocahontas.

John Rolfe: I'm sorry to hear that my white brothers have kidnapped you.

Pocahontas: Don't be sorry. They did not hurt us.

John Rolfe: Good. If anybody ever hurts you, I'll kill him!

Pocahontas: Oh, John, don't be so aggressive! Let's rather think of making peace between your people and mine.

John Rolfe: I'm glad to hear that your father is coming.

Pocahontas: Yes, he can help make peace.

John Rolfe: It's not only that. I have a very important question to ask him.

Pocahontas: Yes?

John Rolfe: But first I have to ask **you** something. *(He kneels down in front of her.)*

Pocahontas: What are you looking for? *(She kneels down, too.)*

John Rolfe: Nothing. I was only going to ask you for your hand.

Pocahontas: My hand? What for?

John Rolfe: Oh, Pocahontas, don't you understand? That is what a white man asks a girl when he wants to marry her.

Pocahontas: Really? I'll have to get used to your strange ways.

John Rolfe: Well, erm ... do you want to marry me?

Pocahontas: I do. But let's stand up. This looks funny. *(She pulls him up by his hands.)*

John Rolfe: Now we must ask your father for permission.

Pocahontas: On our knees?

John Rolfe: Please, Pocahontas, stop kidding. This is serious.

Pocahontas: I know.

Powhatan arrives together with Captain Smith and other settlers.

Captain Smith: Well, Chief, here is your daughter.

Pocahontas: Father! This young man wants me for his wife.

Powhatan: Things are going too fast for me. I thought

my daughter was a prisoner, but now I find out she is a bride.

Captain Smith: And John here is her prisoner – I mean her bridegroom.

Powhatan: What can I say to that?

Captain Smith: Just say "OK", and we've taken a big step towards peace.

Powhatan: That is true. You don't have to fight for things which you can get by love. I have come unarmed, and I am willing to give you what you ask. Believe me, I know that it is better to eat good meat, sleep comfortably, live quietly with my family, laugh and be merry with the Yangis, and be their friend than to fight them and be driven away from my country.

Captain Smith: You are a clever man, Powhatan. War has never solved any problems. We'll have to find a way of living together peacefully and of sharing what the land offers. These two young people could prepare the way.

Powhatan: I hope that you two will be happy, and make your people happy as well.

John Rolfe: I promise.

Captain Smith: So instead of a war, let's have a big feast! Three cheers for the bride and groom!

Cheers. Festive music.

Scene five

1616
Dressed in a lady's splendid gown
The child of nature goes to town.

The home of the Rolfes. Some pieces of furniture (a chair, a small table, a mirror, etc.) show that it is a wealthy house. Pocahontas (now called Rebecca) is trying on a new elegant dress in the style of the early 17th century. Miss Needle is putting pins in her skirt.

Pocahontas: Oooh, it's so terribly tight, I can't even breathe!

Miss Needle: Don't breathe!

Pocahontas: What? I mustn't breathe?

Miss Needle: I mean, don't breathe deeply, like this. *(She shows her.)* If you do, your dress will burst.

Pocahontas: If I don't breathe, I will burst.

Miss Needle: You must behave like a lady, Mrs Rebecca.

Pocahontas: And ladies mustn't breathe?

Miss Needle: No, and they mustn't sneeze either.

Pocahontas: Anything else they mustn't do? *(She wipes her nose on her sleeve.)*

Miss Needle: Yes. Wipe their nose on their sleeve.

Pocahontas: Oh. I'll have to remember. *(She takes a*

cautious step to the mirror.) But how can I walk in this?

Miss Needle: You won't have to walk much. You will ride in a coach and sit on a couch most of the time.

Pocahontas: I'm sure I'll fall over. No wonder, with these shoes! *(She lifts her skirt to show her feet in high-heeled shoes in the style of the early 17th century.)*

Miss Needle: Don't show your feet! A lady never shows her feet in public!

Pocahontas: But I just washed them this morning. And I put on fresh stockings, too.

Miss Needle: I know that. But in high society a lady's feet must not be seen. The only person who is allowed to see them is your husband.

Pocahontas: My husband is the only person who is allowed to see my heart. Anybody may look at my feet!

Miss Needle: Not in high society. They don't want to see anything low.

Rolfe enters.

John Rolfe: Good morning. How is my lady doing? *(He kisses her hand.)*

Pocahontas: Fine, thank you. I mustn't breathe, and I can't walk, but otherwise I'm OK.

John Rolfe: You look wonderful.

Miss Needle: Yes, sir, doesn't she?

John Rolfe: What a lovely dress!

Miss Needle: Beautiful, isn't it?

John Rolfe: Absolutely fantastic. A breathtaking sight.

Pocahontas: It's certainly breathtaking for me.

John Rolfe: Look, I've got a little present for you.

Pocahontas: Oh, thank you. Splendid. Erm – what is it?

John Rolfe: It's a fan. Open it.

Miss Needle: Ladies use it to fan themselves, you know, to get fresh air.

Pocahontas: Oh, I see, so that is how they breathe. *(She fans herself in front of the mirror.)*

Three of the settlers enter, dressed like wealthy gentlemen.

Alan: Good morning, Rebecca, good morning, John.

Barry: My, you look a picture, lady Rebecca.

Charlie: I'm sure you will impress the king of England.

Pocahontas: Thank you, gentlemen. Would you please excuse me? *(She lets each of them kiss her hand and leaves.)*

Barry: You can be proud of your wife, John. She is a lovely lady.

John Rolfe: Thank you, Barry.

Charlie: Well, our colony has become a success story after all.

Barry: And what made us rich? Tobacco!

Alan: OK, OK, so you were right about that taste. And I must admit that I've changed my mind, too. *(He takes out a big cigar and bites off the end.)*

John Rolfe: Please, don't smoke in here, Alan. My wife doesn't like the smell in her drawing-room.

Alan: Oh, of course. Sorry. *(He puts away his cigar.)*

John Rolfe: Well, gentlemen, Rebecca and I will be on our way to merry old England tomorrow. I'm really excited about the trip. *(He pours out drinks.)*

Charlie: I can understand that. Just imagine: meeting King James in person!

Barry: I'm sure the court will love your charming wife.

John Rolfe: Oh yes, but will they love **me**? The king – so I'm told – seems to be unhappy that I've married an Indian princess.

Alan: But why?

John Rolfe: Well, I'm a rich tobacco planter now, but I'm still not an aristocrat by birth.

Charlie: So what? This is Virginia, not Europe.

John Rolfe: Yes, but in Europe people think like this: If Rebecca's father is a true king of this country, then his daughter's husband could claim the country for himself.

Barry: That's ridiculous.

Alan: Not quite. I can see the point: our friend John here is something like a traitor who tries to take away the colony from his king!

Barry: Is that true, John?

John Rolfe: Of course not. I married Rebecca because I love her. I never thought of taking Virginia away from our king.

Alan: Well, gentlemen, here's to the king! *(They raise their glasses.)*

Barry: And here's to lady Rebecca! *(as above)*

Charlie: And here's to our dear friend, John Rolfe! *(same again)*

John Rolfe: Well, gentlemen, it's time to say good-bye.

Alan: We wish you a good journey.

Barry: And a happy return.

John Rolfe: Thank you all.

Charlie: And give our best regards to the royal family!

John Rolfe: I will.

They shake hands with John Rolfe and leave.

John Rolfe: Rebecca!

Pocahontas: Yes, my lord? *(She curtseys.)*

John Rolfe: Don't call me "lord".

Pocahontas: I'm only practising. If I ever fall down in this dress, I'll never be able to get up again.

John Rolfe: Just don't fall.

Pocahontas: I'll do my best.

John Rolfe: I'm sure you'll be OK.

Pocahontas: And you'll be OK, too.

John Rolfe: Let's hope so. Are you looking forward to our trip?

Pocahontas: Yes, very much.

John Rolfe: You know that we'll return to this country one day. Virginia has become our home.

Pocahontas: **Your** home, my dear. It has always been mine.

John Rolfe: Our two worlds have become one. We can show that to the people back in Europe.

Pocahontas:	They might look at my people, the Powhatans, in a different way.
John Rolfe:	Ours is a rich country. There will be peace and plenty for all its inhabitants, Indians and Europeans.
Pocahontas:	Yes, John. Time will tell.

They walk off together. Music of the period.

Epilogue

1622

John Rolfe is sitting at a desk, writing with a quill pen, which he now and then dips into an inkpot. On the wall there is a picture of Pocahontas with a black band around it.

Dear Thomas,

I am writing this to you, my son, to tell you about your dear mother, who died when you were still a little child. You must know that she was an Indian princess by birth. When I first met her she was called Pocahontas by her father, the king of all the Indians of Virginia. When she left the ways of her people and became a good Christian, she took on the name of Rebecca. By marrying her, I believed that a permanent peace could be made between her people and ours. Alas! She died in England when you were only two years old, and within five years of her death a cruel war between the Powhatans and the English colony started. The fighting will surely cost many, many lives on both sides; and it looks like we will never share this country with the red men, but build our farms on the ground where their bones rest.

However, you, my dear son, should always keep in mind that you carry the blood of your Indian mother in you as well as the blood of your European father. Even if the two races did not come together to form a new Christian people on a new continent, I do hope that you at least will combine the best of both races in your person. Show tolerance and kindness as a true Christian, and love the land that was once owned by your mother's people. *(Curtain)*

Chronology

The life of Pocahontas

- 1595? birth of Matoaka, called Pocahontas, daughter of Powhatan
- 1607 traditional story of her rescue of Captain Smith in Werowocomoco; many visits and help to the settlers in Jamestown
- 1612 kidnapping by Captain Samuel Argall
- 1613 conversion to Christianity in Jamestown
- 1614 marriage to John Rolfe, a wealthy tobacco planter
- 1615 birth of their son Thomas
- 1616 trip to England; reception at the court of King James I and Queen Anne
- 1617 death and burial at Gravesend near London
- 1622 death of her husband John Rolfe in Virginia

The early history of American settlement

- 1587 Sir Walter Raleigh sends out 150 colonists to Virginia (where they all perish)
- 1607 first successful settlement in Virginia
- 1614 (April to July) Captain John Smith sails the coast of New England from Maine to Cape Cod
- 1620 settlement of the Pilgrims at Plymouth, Massachusetts
- 1622-44 Powhatan War: The Indians of Virginia are defeated
- 1624 publication of *The General History of Virginia* by Captain Smith

Other historical events of that period

- 1588 the Spanish Armada defeated by the English navy
- 1590-1613 Shakespeare writes his poetry and plays
- 1600 the East India Company is founded
- 1603-25 the reign of King James I
- 1605 Gunpowder Plot of Guy Fawkes
- 1611 King James version of the Bible
- 1618-48 Thirty Years War in Germany

Notes on the text

Prologue
April 26, 1607: On that day, the colonists' three ships (the *Susan Constant*, the *Godspeed* and the *Discovery*) landed in Chesapeake Bay. (The Atlantic crossing, by the way, took them about two months.)

Scene one
Page 9, line 3: Captain Smith himself once tried to catch fish with a frying-pan on an expedition up the Potomac River.

Page 11, line 7: The origin of the word "Yankee" (for "American") is not clear. It probably comes from the natives' pronunciation of the word "English". My personal spelling suggests that the word should be pronounced as a cross between ['ɪŋglɪʃ] and ['jæŋkɪz].

Scene two
Scene 2 is fictitious, but it is recorded that at Pocahontas' deathbed in Gravesend a Powhatan medicine man was present and there might have been some kind of fight over the young woman's spirit with her Christian husband John (cf. Mossiker, p. 297).

Page 19, line 15: Eye-witnesses report that the young Indian "princess" surprised the Europeans by turning cartwheels when she visited their camp.

Scene four
Page 30, line 8: The following text is based on Powhatan's speech at the Indian village of *Werowocomoco* in 1609, as reported by John Smith.

Scene five

Page 35, line 1: Rolfe was the pioneer of tobacco in the Virginian colony (cf. Mossiker, p. 258).

Epilogue

1622: In his last will, written that year, John Rolfe gave 400 acres of land on the James River to his son Thomas. When the Indians attacked the Virginian settlements on March 22 that same year, 347 settlers were killed.

Page 39, line 12 f. (permanent peace): From 1614, the date of Rebecca's marriage, to 1622 the settlers enjoyed a period of peaceful coexistence with the natives, sometimes called the "The Peace of Pocahontas".

Further notes

Did you know that

- Captain John Smith probably came through our country on one of his adventurous trips (that time on his way back from the Orient)?
- King James I considered tobacco to be "a stinking weed" and would not let anyone smoke at court?
- Pocahontas (or rather, Rebecca) was John Rolfe's second wife? His first wife had died in a shipwreck on the way to the colony. In 1619 Rolfe got married again and had a daughter with his third wife.
- about 2 million Americans in Virginia claim to be descended from Pocahontas?
- even President Thomas Jefferson believed to be a descendant of the Indian princess?
- the first stage play (1784) about our heroine was written by a German named Johann Wilhelm Rose?
- since then about 50 stage plays (including this one) have been written on that subject?
- today only a few so-called Powhatans still live in Virginia, recognized by the government as an "Indian tribe"?

Vocabulary

pl. = plural, *n.* = noun, *sb.* = somebody, *sth.* = something, *infml.* = informal

A **absolutely fantastic** [ˌæbsəluːtli fæn'tæstɪk] ganz fantastisch
acre ['eɪkə] Landfläche von 4047 qm
(to) **admit** [əd'mɪt] zugeben
adventurous [əd'ventʃərəs] abenteuerlich
aggressive [ə'gresɪv] aggressiv, angriffslustig
alas! [ə'læs] aber ach!
Algonquian [æl'gɒŋkwiən] Algonkin *(Sprache des Algonkin-Indianerstammes)*
alias ['eɪliəs] alias
(to) **approach** [ə'prəʊtʃ] näherkommen
aristocrat ['ærɪstəkræt] Aristokrat/in, Adlige/r
arms *(pl.)* [ɑːmz] Waffen

B **background** ['bækgraʊnd] Hintergrund
(to) **bang** [bæŋ] schlagen
(to) **bargain** ['bɑːgən] verhandeln
based on: (to) **be based on** [beɪst] beruhen auf
(to) **behave** [bɪ'heɪv] sich verhalten
berry ['beri] Beere
Bible ['baɪbl] Bibel
birth: **by birth** [bɜːθ] von Geburt
(to) **bite off, bit, bitten** [baɪt, bɪt, 'bɪtn] abbeißen
blood [blʌd] Blut
bone [bəʊn] Knochen
brave [breɪv] mutig
(to) **breathe** [briːð] atmen
breathtaking ['breθteɪkɪŋ] atemberaubend

bride [braɪd] Braut
bridegroom ['braɪdgru:m] Bräutigam
burial ['beriəl] Beerdigung, Beisetzung
(to) **burst, burst, burst** [bɜ:st] bersten, platzen

C **campfire** ['kæmpfaɪə] Lagerfeuer
(to) **care for sb.** [keə] jn. mögen, gut leiden können
(to) **carry on** [ˌkæri‿'ɒn] weitersprechen
(to) **carry out** [ˌkæri‿'aʊt] erfüllen, ausführen
(to) **catch, caught, caught** [kætʃ, kɔ:t] *hier:* mitkriegen, verstehen
cautious ['kɔ:ʃəs] vorsichtig
(to) **change one's mind** [maɪnd] seine Meinung ändern
charming ['tʃɑ:mɪŋ] charmant, bezaubernd
cheer: three cheers for the bride [tʃɪəz], [braɪd] ein dreifaches Hoch für die Braut
Christianity [ˌkrɪsti'ænəti] Christentum
cigar [sɪ'gɑ:] Zigarre
(to) **claim** [kleɪm] beanspruchen; behaupten
coach [kəʊtʃ] Kutsche
coexistence [ˌkəʊɪg'zɪstəns] Zusammenleben, Koexistenz
(to) **combine** [kəm'baɪn] vereinigen
completely [kəm'pli:tli] völlig
(to) **consider** [kən'sɪdə] betrachten, halten für
(to) **console** [kən'səʊl] trösten
conversion [kən'vɜ:ʃn] Bekehrung, Konversion
corn-cob ['kɔ:n kɒb] Maiskolben
couch [kaʊtʃ] Sofa
court [kɔ:t] (Königs-)Hof
(to) **curtsey** ['kɜ:tsi] einen Knicks machen

D **deathbed** ['deθbed] Totenbett
(to) **defend** [dɪ'fend] verteidigen
descendant [dɪ'sendənt] Nachkomme
descended: be descended from [dɪ'sendɪd] abstammen von
devil ['devl] Teufel
(to) **dig up** [ˌdɪg‿'ʌp] ausgraben
(to) **dip** [dɪp] eintauchen
dove [dʌv] Taube
drawing-room ['drɔːɪŋ ruːm] Wohnzimmer
(to) **drive away** [ˌdraɪv‿ə'weɪ] vertreiben
(to) **drop** [drɒp] fallen lassen; fallen
drum [drʌm] Trommel

E **eagle** ['iːgl] Adler
earth [ɜːθ] Erde
elegant ['elɪgənt] elegant
(to) **embrace** [ɪm'breɪs] sich umarmen
(to) **end** [end] enden, aufhören
eyewitness ['aɪwɪtnəs] Augenzeuge, Augenzeugin

F **fan** [fæn] Fächer
(to) **fan** [fæn] sich Luft zufächeln
feast [fiːst] Fest, Festessen
feather ['feðə] Feder
festive ['festɪv] festlich
fictitious [fɪk'tɪʃəs] erfunden, fiktiv
followers ['fɒləʊəz] Gefolgsleute
forehead ['fɔːhed] Stirn
(to) **form** [fɔːm] bilden
frying-pan ['fraɪɪŋ pæn] Bratpfanne

G **game** [geɪm] Wild
gentle ['dʒentl] zart
(to) **get on sb.'s nerves** [nɜːvz] jm. auf die Nerven gehen
(to) **get out** *hier:* verschwinden
(to) **get used to sth.** [juːst] sich an etw. gewöhnen
go ahead, ...! [ə'hed] nur zu, ...!
good: for good [fə 'gʊd] ein für allemal
gown [gaʊn] Kleid
(to) **grab** [græb] ergreifen
greedy ['griːdi] habgierig
guess: I guess [ges] ich nehme an, ich denke

H (to) **hand** [hænd] geben, reichen
headdress ['heddres] Kopfputz, -schmuck
(to) **heal** [hiːl] heilen
heart [hɑːt] Herz
heaven ['hevn] Himmel
hell! *(infml.)* [hel] so'n Mist!, zum Teufel!
herb tea [ˌhɜːb 'tiː] Kräutertee
heroine ['herəʊɪn] (Titel-)Heldin
(to) **hesitate** ['hezɪteɪt] zögern
high society [ˌhaɪ sə'saɪeti] gehobene Gesellschaft
high-heeled [ˌhaɪ 'hiːld] hochhackig
hocus-pocus [ˌhəʊkəs 'pəʊkəs] Hokuspokus
homeland ['həʊmlænd] Heimat(land)
howgh [haʊ] gut
(to) **hunt** [hʌnt] jagen
hunt *(n.)* [hʌnt] Jagd
hush! [hʌʃ] still!

I (to) **impress** [ɪm'pres] beeindrucken
including [ɪn'kluːdɪŋ] einschließlich

inhabitant [ɪn'hæbɪtənt] Bewohner/in, Einwohner/in
inkpot ['ɪŋkpɒt] Tintenfass

J **jar** [dʒɑː] (irdenes) Gefäß

K (to) **keep in mind** [maɪnd] in Erinnerung behalten
kettle ['ketl] Kessel
(to) **kid** [kɪd] herumalbern
kindness ['kaɪndnəs] Güte
(to) **kiss** [kɪs] küssen
(to) **kneel down** [ˌniːl 'daʊn] niederknien

L **last will** [lɑːst 'wɪl] Testament
leather ['leðə] Leder
(to) **lie, lied, lied** [laɪ, laɪd] lügen
(to) **look sb. over** jn. von oben bis unten betrachten
louse, *pl.:* **lice** [laʊs, laɪs] Laus
luck [lʌk] Glück

M **marriage** ['mærɪdʒ] Hochzeit, Heirat
missionary ['mɪʃənri] Missionar/in

N **native** ['neɪtɪv] Eingeborene/r
nature ['neɪtʃə] Natur
navy ['neɪvi] Marine

O **ornament** ['ɔːnəmənt] Schmuck
otherwise ['ʌðəwaɪz] davon abgesehen
own: on one's own [əʊn] selbst, (von) allein

P **patient** ['peɪʃnt] Patient/in
period ['pɪəriəd] Periode, Zeitraum
(to) **perish** ['perɪʃ] umkommen, sterben
permanent ['pɜːmənənt] dauerhaft
pin [pɪn] Stecknadel
pioneer [ˌpaɪə'nɪə] Pionier
pipe [paɪp] Pfeife
plain [pleɪn] einfach
planter ['plɑːntə] Pflanzer/in
plenty ['plenti] Fülle, Reichtum
(to) **point at** [pɔɪnt] zeigen auf
(to) **pour** [pɔː] einschenken
(to) **pray** [preɪ] beten
prayer [preə] Gebet
(to) **present** [prɪ'zent] präsentieren, zeigen
promise ['prɒmɪs] Versprechen
public: in public ['pʌblɪk] in der Öffentlichkeit
publication [ˌpʌblɪ'keɪʃn] Veröffentlichung

Q **quill pen** [ˌkwɪl 'pen] Feder(kiel)

R **race** [reɪs] Rasse
(to) **raise** [reɪz] aufziehen; anbauen; erheben
rather ['rɑːðə] vielmehr
(to) **rattle a gourd** [ˌrætl‿ə 'gʊəd] rasseln (mit einem ausgehöhlten Kürbis)
rear [rɪə] hinterer Teil
reception [rɪ'sepʃn] Empfang
redskin ['redskɪn] Rothaut
(to) **reduce the fever** [rɪˌdjuːs ðə 'fiːvə] das Fieber senken
(to) **refuse** [rɪ'fjuːz] zurückweisen
reign [reɪn] Regentschaft

rescue ['reskju:] Rettung, Befreiung
(to) **rest** [rest] ruhen
return [rɪ'tɜ:n] Rückkehr
ridiculous [rɪ'dɪkjələs] lächerlich
root [ru:t] Wurzel
rope [rəʊp] Strick
(to) **rule** [ru:l] herrschen

S **scalp** [skælp] Skalp
scout [skaʊt] Kundschafter
shipwreck ['ʃɪprek] Schiffbruch
shocked [ʃɒkt] geschockt
(to) **shut up** *(infml.)* [ˌʃʌt_'ʌp] den Mund halten
since then [sɪns 'ðen] seitdem
signboard ['saɪnbɔ:d] Tafel
single: not a single one ['sɪŋgl] nicht ein/e einzige/r
(to) **sneeze** [sni:z] niesen
so-called ['səʊ kɔ:ld] sogenannt
sole [səʊl] Sohle
(to) **solve** [sɒlv] *(Aufgabe, Problem)* lösen
speech [spi:tʃ] Rede
spirit ['spɪrɪt] Geist
splendid ['splendɪd] prächtig
squaw [skwɔ:] Frau *(Wort der Algonkinsprache)*
stage [steɪdʒ] Bühne
stage props ['steɪdʒ prɒps] Requisiten
stake [steɪk] (Marter-)Pfahl
step [step] Schritt
stew [stju:] Eintopf
stinking weed [ˌstɪŋkɪŋ 'wi:d] Stinkkraut
stocking ['stɒkɪŋ] Strumpf
(to) **stop sb. from doing sth.** jn. davon abhalten, etw. zu tun
(to) **strike, struck, struck** [straɪk, strʌk] zuschlagen

stuff *(infml.)* [stʌf] Zeug
(to) **stuff** [stʌf] stopfen
subject ['sʌbdʒɪkt] Thema
success [sək'ses] Erfolg
succotash ['sʌkətæʃ] ein Gericht aus Bohnen und Mais *(Wort der Algonkinsprache)*
(to) **survive** [sə'vaɪv] überleben

T (to) **take on** annehmen
(to) **take turns** [ˌteɪk 'tɜːnz] sich abwechseln
taste [teɪst] Geschmack
tear [tɪə] Träne
(to) **tie sb. up** [ˌtaɪ‿'ʌp] jn. fesseln
tired: be tired of ['taɪəd] (etwas) satt haben, genug haben von
tobacco [tə'bækəʊ] Tabak
tolerance ['tɒlərəns] Toleranz
traitor ['treɪtə] Verräter/in
trance [trɑːns] Trance, schlafähnlicher Zustand
(to) **trust sb.** [trʌst] jm. vertrauen
(to) **turn a cartwheel** [ˌtɜːn‿ə 'kɑːtwiːl] ein Rad schlagen

U **unarmed** [ˌʌn'ɑːmd] unbewaffnet
unless [ən'les] wenn … nicht, außer wenn, es sei denn
(to) **untie sb.** [ʌn'taɪ] jn. losbinden

V **version** ['vɜːʃn] Fassung

W (to) **want sb. to do sth.** wollen, dass jn. etw. tut
warrior ['wɒriə] Krieger/in

wealthy ['welθi] wohlhabend, reich
whatever [wɒt'evə] egal, ganz gleich was
which art [wɪtʃ‿'ɑːt] du bist *(Anfang des Vaterunsers = the Lord's Prayer)*
wigwam ['wɪgwæm] Wigwam *(Algonkinwort für Hütte, Behausung)*
willing: be willing to sth. ['wɪlɪŋ] bereit sein, etw. zu tun
willow bark ['wɪləʊ bɑːk] Weidenrinde *(ein indianisches Fieberheilmittel)*
wingapoh [ˌwɪŋgə'puː] *freundliche Begrüßung in der Algonkinsprache*
(to) **wipe one's nose on one's sleeve** [waɪp], [sliːv] sich die Nase am Ärmel abputzen
within [wɪ'ðɪn] innerhalb, in
(to) **wonder** ['wʌndə] sich fragen, gerne wissen wollen
wonder ['wʌndə] Wunder

Names

People's names

Alan ['ælən]
Barry ['bæri]
Captain Smith [ˌkæptɪn 'smɪθ]
Charlie ['tʃɑːli]
David ['deɪvɪd]
Edward ['edwəd]
Francis ['frɑːnsɪs]
George [dʒɔːdʒ]
Harry ['hæri]
John Rolfe [ˌdʒɒn 'rɒlf]
Matachanna [mætə'tʃænə]
Matoaka [mætə'(w)ɑːkə]
Miss Needle [ˌmɪs 'niːdl]
Pocahontas [ˌpɒkə'hɒntəs]
Powhatan [paʊə'tæn]
Rebecca [rɪ'bekə]
Wassuhonacock [wɒsə'hɔnəkɔk]

Place names

Jamestown ['dʒeɪmztaʊn]
Tidewater ['taɪdwɔːtə]
Virginia [və'dʒɪniə]

Bibliography

- Mossiker, Frances. Pocahontas. The Life and the Legend. New York: Knopf, 1976
- Tilton, Robert S. Pocahontas. The Evolution of an American Narrative. Cambridge: Cambridge University Press, 1994
- Woodward, Grace Steele. Pocahontas. Norman: University of Oklahoma Press, 1969